Gift to the

EVANSTON·PUBLIC
LIBRARY

IN MEMORY

OF

MRS. TAFT

Gift Book Fund

Olympic Peninsula

The Grace & Grandeur

Mike Sedam

Voyageur Press | *A Pictorial* *Discovery* Guide

Page 1:
This small stream trickles through the Quinault Rain Forest. The three main rain forest valleys on the western Olympic slope—Hoh, Queets, and Quinault—average twelve feet of moisture per year. Fog also adds to the moisture content.

Pages 2–3:
Thousands of years of wave action carved Split Rock on Rialto Beach in Olympic National Park. This view is from Hole-in-the-Wall Headland.

Pages 6–7:
Ruby Beach, located on the longest stretch of wild coastline in the coterminous United States, is protected as a part of Olympic National Park. Ruby is known for its spectacular sea stacks, the largest of which is Abbey Island, pictured to the left in this image.

Text and photographs © 2002 by Mike Sedam

Edited by Kari Cornell
Designed by Maria Friedrich
Printed in China

02   03   04   05   06   5   4   3   2   1

Library of Congress Cataloging-in-Publication Data

Sedam, Mike.
  Olympic Peninsula : the grace & grandeur / Mike Sedam.
    p. cm. — (A pictorial discovery guide)
Includes bibliographical references (p. 140) and index.
  ISBN 0-89658-458-5 (hardcover)
  1. Olympic Peninsula (Wash.)—Pictorial works. 2. Olympic Peninsula (Wash.)—Description and travel. 3. Olympic Peninsula (Wash.)—Guidebooks. I. Title. II. Series.
  F897.O5 S43 2002
  917.97'940444—dc21

                                        2002005223

Distributed in Canada by Raincoast Books, 9050 Shaughnessy Street, Vancouver, B.C. V6P 6E5

Published by Voyageur Press, Inc.
123 North Second Street, P.O. Box 338, Stillwater, MN 55082 U.S.A.
651-430-2210, fax 651-430-2211
books@voyageurpress.com
www.voyageurpress.com

Educators, fundraisers, premium and gift buyers, publicists, and marketing managers: Looking for creative products and new sales ideas? Voyageur Press books are available at special discounts when purchased in quantities, and special editions can be created to your specifications. For details contact the marketing department at 800-888-9653.

Olympic Peninsula

Tatoosh Island
Cape Flattery — Neah Bay
Makah Indian Reservation

Deception Pass State Park ■

Whidbey Island

Sekui
Clallam Bay
Shi Shi Beach
Point of Arches
Cape Alava
Flattery Rocks Nat'l Wildlife Refuge
Ozette (village)

Strait of Juan de Fuca
Salt Creek
Olympic National Park

Dungeness Nat'l Wildlife Refuge
Dungeness Spit
Ediz Hook
Port Angeles
Sequim
Port Townsend

Lake Crescent
Aldwell Lake

Lake Ozette

Rialto Beach
La Push

Quillayute Needles Nat'l Wildlife Refuge

Sol Duc River
Bogachiel River
Forks

Marymere Falls
Olympic Hot Springs
Sol Duc Hot Springs
Sol Duc Falls

Heart O' the Hills
Chimacum
Admiralty Inlet
Marrowstone Island

Hurricane Ridge

Dungeness River

Quilcene
Port Gamble

Bailey Range

▲ *Mount Olympus*

Elwah River

Hoh River
Hoh Rain Forest

Olympic Coast National Marine Sanctuary

Ruby Beach

Queets River
Quinault River

Dosewallips River
Enchanted Valley
Brinnon

Hood Canal
Old Man House State Park

Kalaloch Beach
Queets

Graves Creek

Seattle ↗
Bremerton
Puget Sound

Quinault Indian Reservation

Falls Creek
Lake Quinault
Lake Cushman

Skokomish River

Kitsap Peninsula

Pacific Ocean

Moclips
Pacific Beach

Union

Tacoma

Copalis Beach
Ocean City
Highway 101

Ocean Shores
Hoquiam
Highway 12
Aberdeen
Cosmopolis
Grays Harbor

Chehalis River

Olympia
Tumwater

Contents

Introduction

My first memories of the Olympic Peninsula were shaped right around the time of my sixteenth birthday. I had just earned my driver's license and gotten my first car. At the time, I was working weekends and after school as a bus boy in the Seattle-Tacoma International Airport dining room. I needed a good job to feed my need for a car, camera equipment, film, processing, and darkroom supplies. I had taken a photography class at school the year before, thinking it would be an easy class. Now I was spending whatever free time I had shooting pictures or developing them in the darkroom at Mt. Rainier High School.

One Sunday, a photograph in the *Seattle Times* caught my eye. The picture, taken by Bob and Ira Spring, was of Lake Crescent as seen from U.S. Highway 101, the road that circles the Olympic Peninsula. In the 1960s, the Springs pioneered scenic photography in the Northwest, and their images were everywhere. One of their photographs and a short column was featured each week in the Rotogravure section of the *Seattle Times*. As I remember it, each week's photo highlighted a different location, usually in western Washington. The Rotogavure section was the main reason I read the paper. In fact, it was the work of the Springs, Ansel Adams, and Alfred Stieglitz that inspired me to pursue a career as a professional photographer.

I did a little research and found out where the Springs had taken the image of Lake Crescent. About two weeks after buying my very first car, a 1951 Dodge four-door sedan, I decided to visit this very inspirational place. I wanted to take a picture from the same place that the famous Springs had taken a shot. The problem was, I didn't have the time to drive 420 miles around the peninsula. Between high school, my job at the airport, and a few other activities, I had no free days. So, I did what any enterprising teenage kid with the newfound freedom of his first car would do: I decided to go at night.

The next Friday I followed my usual schedule—I went to school and then I worked my 3:00 P.M. to 12:00 A.M. shift at the airport. Then I loaded my camera equipment into the back of my car and set out on my first all-night photo shoot. I learned a lot that night. I found out that even teenagers can get tired of driving, that it rains a lot on the peninsula, that my car burned more gas than I thought, and that my parents would get very upset if I stayed out all night without telling them in advance. And I knew they would not approve of my driving that old wreck of a car such a long way from home.

"What if it had broken down in the middle of the night? What would you have done?" they had asked later.

My only response was "It didn't break down."

After this incident, I lost my newfound freedom for a month. But I discovered something else during that trip that made it all worthwhile: I love the peninsula. Since that fateful midnight drive, it has been my privilege and pleasure to explore and capture the wild beauty of the Olympic Peninsula. During the past thirty-two years, I have photographed the peninsula's deep forests, glaciered pinnacles, abundant and unique wildlife, and wild, windy coast. I have experienced the rainy days and gazed up at night skies full of stars. And I have discovered that change is inevitable on the peninsula. The sea and the land are constantly engaged in a slow battle for dominance. Over the centuries, plants and animals have had to adapt in order to thrive in this unique environment. In making the images in this book, I simply celebrated the adventure of experiencing this astounding place. With this book, I encourage you to take the adventure yourself.

Lake Crescent can be a very peaceful place at sunset.

The Olympic Peninsula

The Olympic Peninsula, located only a half day's drive from the busy and overcrowded streets of Seattle, attracts many visitors each year. Situated in the far northwest corner of the state of Washington, the peninsula holds one of the last great wilderness areas left in the continental United States. Bound by the great Pacific Ocean in the west, the picturesque Strait of Juan de Fuca in the north, Puget Sound and the Kitsap Peninsula to the east, and the Chehalis River to the south, the Olympic is home to one of the finest temperate rain forests in the world. Ice-cold rivers holding seven species of salmon, spectacular waterfalls, and snow-covered alpine peaks also grace this land. The Olympic Peninsula is famous for breathtaking glaciers and an abundance of wildlife, including the Roosevelt elk and at least eight types of plants and eighteen types of animals that are found nowhere else on Earth. At the heart of the peninsula, the most pristine part of the wilderness is preserved within Olympic National Park.

The park features three distinct ecosystems: the Olympic Mountains, old-growth rain forest valleys, and the rugged, Pacific coast. Access to the peninsula's interior by road is limited, but nearly 600 miles of hiking trails crisscross the park.

Olympic National Park contains the largest and best example of virgin temperate rain forest in the Western Hemisphere, the largest intact stand of coniferous forest in the lower forty-eight states, and the largest herd of Roosevelt elk, consisting of nearly 5,000 animals. Approximately sixty miles of spectacular, undeveloped coastline and many offshore islands and sea stacks make the park's coastline unique.

The park contains one of the most well-preserved ecosystems in the contiguous United States, featuring more than 1,200 plants, such as conifers and wildflowers, more than 300 species of birds, and more than 70 species of mammals. Thirteen major rivers and 200 smaller streams provide a rich habitat for fish and other aquatic creatures.

History of the Peninsula

"When the tide is out, the table is set." This old proverb of early inhabitants of the Olympic Peninsula coastline speaks volumes about their way of life. The earliest evidence of humans on the Olympic Peninsula dates from 6,000 to 9,000 years ago, when the Quinault, Hoh, Quillayute, Makah, Klallam, Chimacum, and Skokomish people first made this area home. These groups set up camps along the coasts during the summer months, digging for shellfish on the beach and fishing for salmon, halibut, bottom fish, whale, and porpoise from hollowed-out red cedar canoes. These early inhabitants depended on the Pacific Ocean and the riches it provided to survive.

Follow the Shipwreck Coast Trail 1.6 miles to the Hole-in-the-Wall Headland. True to its name, Hole-in-the-Wall is a large hole in the rock, worn through by thousands of years of wave action.

Many of these Native Americans lived in longhouses, large wooden buildings—some as long as sixty feet—constructed of red cedar logs and boards. Between four and six extended families lived in each house. These houses could be disassembled and moved to another location if necessary. In the winter, the people of the coast often relocated inland to set up camp in the foothills, where they would hunt for elk and deer. The native groups lived undisturbed on the peninsula until the arrival of European explorers.

European Explorers Arrive

In 1592, Apostolos Varianos (nicknamed Juan de Fuca by the Spanish), a Greek explorer sailing under the Spanish flag, claimed to have found the entrance to Puget Sound. An account of his discovery, published in 1625, described his journey from Spanish-held Acapulco, Mexico, north to the Strait of Juan de Fuca. Rumors of de Fuca's discovery prompted other explorers to come to the area.

In 1778, English Captain James Cook sailed past the northwestern tip of the Olympic Peninsula, naming it Cape Flattery. But Cook missed the opening to the Strait of Juan de Fuca. Less than ten years later in 1787, Captain Charles Barkley, an English fur trader, sailed the strait with his ship *Imperial Eagle*. He traveled with his wife Frances Hornby Trevor, who became the first European woman to visit the Northwest coast.

Sitka spruce, rising like pillars from the lush forest floor, frame the Rain Forest Nature Trail located near Lake Quinault. In the rain forest climate, mosses, ferns, and conifer seedlings carpet every available spot, including fallen nurse logs and standing stumps.

In the spring of 1792, the English explorer Captain George Vancouver, who was in search of a Northwest passage, sailed his sloop *Discovery* and the armed tender *Chatham* along the Washington coastline and into the strait. He named the sheltered harbor in which he and his crew landed Port Discovery after his ship, and he appropriately named the small island guarding the entrance Protection Island.

While at anchor there, Vancouver set out in two small boats for further exploration of the vicinity. He sailed into the nearby harbor and named it Port Townsend, in honor of the Marquis of Townsend. Captain Vancouver explored and charted the entire Puget Sound region. He named Hood Canal, the Olympic Mountains, and many other landmarks on the peninsula.

Exploration of the Interior

Few Europeans explored beyond the beaches of the peninsula for the next one hundred years. The first overland crossing of the peninsula didn't occur until 1878, when Melbourne Watkinson and four other men crossed near Lake Cushman and into the upper east fork of the Quinault River before descending to Lake Quinault. The explorers canoed to the ocean from Lake Quinault, guided by a group of American Indians.

In an attempt to cross the Olympic Mountains, Lieutenant Joseph O'Neil led a party in 1885, but they turned around and returned to base camp without crossing the Olympic Range. In 1890, O'Neil lead his second expedition, this time crossing the Olympic Range.

On October 17, 1889, just before the second O'Neil expedition, the father-and-son team of Charles and Samuel Gilman set out from Grays Harbor.

The pair traveled along the beach to the mouth of the Quinault River, where, with the help of the Native Americans, they canoed up the river to Lake Quinault. At the lake they met several European trappers who trapped the surrounding area for furs. The Gilmans continued hiking up the east fork of the Quinault River into Enchanted Valley where they climbed a nearby peak for a view of Hood Canal, Mount Olympus, and the Cascades. But bad weather prevented the Gilmans from traveling any farther.

In the fall of 1889, the Washington territorial governor and the *Seattle Press* took a great interest in the exploration of the interior, sponsoring a group called the Press Expedition. James Helborl Christie led six other hearty souls across the Olympic Mountains. They would attempt a north-south crossing beginning at the Elwha River and ending at Lake Quinault. They left Port Angeles in December 1889, during harsh winter weather, which impeded their progress. They arrived at Lake Quinault on May 21, some six months after they had begun, achieving the first documented crossing of the Olympics. Today, visitors to Olympic National Park often hike the same route in only about six days. Established trails, good maps, and decent weather make all the difference.

Settling the Peninsula

The first settlers to come to the peninsula established homesteads and farms along the northern coastal areas in 1853. The community known as Chimacum was established ten miles south of Port Townsend where the Center Valley and the East Valley meet. Reuben S. Robinson was the first to settle in the valleys, followed by William Bishop and William Eldridge who claimed land along Chimacum Creek. Bishop and Eldridge had abandoned the *Monarch*, a British man-of-war anchored near Victoria. Five other sailors from the ship joined Bishop and Eldridge, hiring a Native American guide to row them across the Strait of Juan de Fuca to North Beach near Port Townsend.

Due to poor drainage in the area, crops didn't do well, so Bishop and Eldridge took up dairy farming. Their butter and cheese were sold as far away as Seattle and Tacoma; they even became award-winning Holstein breeders.

Marrowstone Island, located just southeast of Port Townsend in Puget Sound, was also settled by farmers. Turkeys were the "crop" of choice in the beginning, but when growers discovered that the more profitable strawberry seemed to flourish in the island's rich soil, planting fields of

Mountain goats were introduced to Olympic National Park in 1924, when twelve mountain goats were released. By 1995, the population had grown to about 1,200 animals. The park service had to remove most of the goat population because of the severe damage they inflicted on the native vegetation.

the sweet red berries became more popular. This area is still known for its strawberries, and the island hosts a strawberry festival each June.

People settled the rain forests of the western coastal area of the peninsula—including the Hoh, Queets, and Quinault river valleys and the surrounding rain forests—between 1893 and 1898. At this time, economic depression seized the Northwest, and there were few jobs available in the cities. To the prospective settlers, a chance to own their own land must have seemed like the only way out of the bad economic situation.

The Homestead Act, passed in 1862, and the Timber and Stone Act, passed in 1878, enabled anyone to acquire land and develop it. A settler merely had to stake claim to land and work the plot for five years to earn the title to 160 acres.

Homesteaders traveled by steamer to Pysht (a settlement which no longer exists along the Pysht River), Clallam Bay, or Neah Bay. From these settlements they hired Native American guides to transport them south in dugout canoes. Others came by beach trail. By the early 1900s, settlers had established ranches in the river valleys. Most were subsistence farmers. Those who chose to live in the rain forest had no choice but to live as part of it. Lack of roads made it difficult to get anything but livestock to market in Port Townsend. Homesteaders earned cash any way they could in order to pay taxes and buy foods they could not produce themselves, such as flour, coffee, and sugar.

One of the most renowned pioneers of the area was John Huelsdonk (1867–1946), the "Iron Man of the Hoh." He was portrayed as a man with legendary prowess beyond the capacity of the average human. Huelsdonk lived on the Hoh River, raised cattle and sheep, gardened, trapped, hunted bounty animals, and carried backpacks for hunters, geologists, loggers, and surveyors.

Huelsdonk became famous when he was seen on the trail carrying a cookstove on his back. Someone asked him about the heavy load, and he replied that the stove by itself wasn't so bad, it was the sack of flour inside the thing, which shifted from side to side as he walked, that made the stove difficult to haul. This story made its way into the national publications of the time, including *Time* and the *Saturday Evening Post*.

Official settlement of the peninsula occurred in the late 1800s and early 1900s. Washington became a state in 1889, and between 1897 and 1911, the federal government built Fort Casey, Fort Flagler, and Fort Worden to protect the Puget Sound Naval Shipyard in Bremerton and the other cities that banked Puget Sound. At the time they were built, these forts had the most modern weapons and fortifications ever designed. It's said that guns at Fort Worden were so accurate that they could hit the smokestack of any enemy ship bent on trying to enter Puget Sound. The three forts formed the so-called "triangle of death," for their armaments would deliver certain death to any invading enemy.

A second wave of settlers—loggers, hunters, and trappers—came to use the forest, not to live in it. The first detailed government report of the area, released in 1897, stated: "The cost of clearing the forest disqualifies the area for agriculture because no farm land is worth such a price. The most expensive item is getting rid of rotten and decaying wood, which never dries. For logging, however, the land would be ideal."

And log they did. The Quinault, Hoh, Bogachiel, and Queets forests were saved, mainly because the railroad necessary to transport the logs to market never materialized. By the time the logging industry solved the transportation problem, the federal government had established Mount Olympus National Monument, and most of the area in question fell within the new park's protected boundaries. The monument later became Olympic National Park, where logging was banned for good. The timber industry, the United States Forest Service, and even the National Park Service have on many occasions tried to remove some of the more valuable sections of the rain forests from the protection afforded them by their designation as protected lands. For the most part, these attempts fail.

The loggers brought with them the practice of market hunting for elk. The animals were hunted and sold for their meat in and around cities such as Seattle, Port Townsend, Tacoma, and Hoquiam. Hunting elk was a much cheaper way of getting meat than raising cattle on a

From Hurricane Ridge looking southwest toward the Elwha River Valley and the Bailey Range, visitors are able to see the Hurricane Ridge Visitor Center. Hurricane Ridge is the most visited place in Olympic National Park. The ridge gets its name from the high winds that sometimes blow here from the southwest. The winds can be exceptionally strong during the winter months.

Sol Duc Falls, viewed here from the bridge that crosses the canyon just below the falls, is one of the largest and most beautiful waterfalls in Olympic National Park. To reach the falls, visitors walk through an old-growth forest of hemlocks and Douglas firs. Some of these trees are more than twenty feet in circumference and 300 years of age.

farm. By 1903, however, fewer that 500 elk remained on the entire peninsula. In 1905, the state legislature passed a law that prohibited the killing of elk anywhere in the state, and herds began to slowly regenerate. As of 1999, there were approximately 5,000 elk residing in Olympic National Park alone.

As World War I began, the army required large quantities of Sitka spruce for airplane construction. Spruce was used because of the wood's exceptional strength and its relatively low weight. The United States Army sent 30,000 "spruce soldiers" to the peninsula to build a railroad and the world's largest sawmill. This plan included the logging of the choice spruce from the rain forest valleys, but the war ended just before the railroad and the sawmill were completed. Had the war not ended when it did, most of the giant Sitka spruce of the Olympic rain forests may have been used to build the airplanes that flew over Germany and France.

Tourism Comes to the Peninsula

Tourism boomed on the Olympic Peninsula at the turn of the century, and Lake Crescent was the main attraction. In 1890, when the first homesteaders arrived at the lake, they immediately found a market for guiding fishermen, hikers, and hunters. Paul Barns, the brother of Charles Barns, a member of the original Press Expedition, ran the first excursion boat on the lake in 1891. The county later added ferryboats, which provided the main form of transportation in the area until the road along U.S. Highway 101 was completed in 1922.

Singer's Tavern opened on the south shore of Lake Crescent near Barns Point in 1915. President Franklin Roosevelt stayed at the inn during his trip to inspect the area for possible designation as a national park. Singer's Tavern has since been renamed Lake Crescent Lodge. It's open between the last Saturday in April and the last Sunday in October each year.

Early in the 1900s, two hot springs—Sol Duc Hot Springs and the Olympic Hot Springs—were touted for their medicinal value. Folks from Seattle made the three-to-five-day journey by boat and wagon to spend a week. Tourists would arrive in Port Angeles or Port Crescent on the "Mosquito Fleet" (the independent ferries that operated in Puget Sound) and then travel by wagon through the forest to the Olympic Hot Springs in the Elwha River Valley or to the Sol Duc Hot Springs in the Sol Duc River Valley.

The most famous resort of the time was Qui Si Sana which means "here get well" in Latin. The owner was a German-born naturopathic physician named Louis Dechmann who provided guests with 60-degree baths, vinegar wraps, and open-air cabins. The doctor guaranteed good health through diet, exercise, hydrotherapy, and radium treatments. The resort closed in 1918 because some people thought that Dechmann, who

raised the German flag above the American flag at Lake Crescent, favored Germany in the war.

The Pacific coastal areas to the west opened to tourism much later than Lake Crescent and the hot springs resorts. But when U.S. Highway 101 connected Lake Quinault and Hoquiam in 1915, the Log Hotel on Lake Quinault was ready and waiting. Built in the 1880s, the hotel offered a warm bed and good food for those hardy enough to endure the journey on horseback. Then, in August 1924, like so many other lodges of the time, the Log Hotel burned to the ground. In August 1926, the Lake Quinault Lodge opened. The lodge still stands, looking much as it did in 1926. It's the only lodge actually located in one of the valley rain forests. Although the lodge is not in Olympic National Park, it is in Olympic National Forest.

In the 1920s, Charles W. Becker built Becker's Inn and Resort Cabins (now Kalaloch Lodge) on the Pacific coast near Kalaloch Creek. At the time, no roads led to the lodge. In 1931, when the Olympic Loop Highway (U.S. Highway 101) was completed, ribbon-cutting ceremonies for the new road were held here. Today, Kalaloch Lodge is the only year-round lodging available in Olympic National Park.

With the completion of Highway 101, several new resorts, known as auto camps, opened in the 1930s. During the Great Depression, these coastal resorts offered simple wood-frame cottages at a reasonable price. Today, none of these auto camps survive.

The end of World War II brought tourists to the peninsula in droves. It was during this time that many of the peninsula's cabins, campgrounds, lodges, motels, and other facilities were built. Today, more than 3.5 million people visit Olympic National Park each year. Olympic Peninsula tourism has blossomed into an industry worth hundreds of millions of dollars annually.

Establishment of the Park

In 1897, President Grover Cleveland set aside 2,188,800 acres of forestland, including most of the Olympic Mountains, for the establishment of the Olympic Forest Reserve. Explorer Judge James Wickersham was sent to survey the land before the reserve boundaries were determined. Wickersham noted that since the majority of the new reserve lands were far from tidewater, the land was of no use to logging companies. In the 1890s, timber that was high in the mountains was considered inaccessible because there was no easy way to transport the logs to the mills.

By 1901, a proclamation by President William McKinley reduced the size of the Olympic Forest Reserve by 721,920 acres. The land removed from protection included some of the best land for logging in the reserve. A visit to the peninsula in 1908 prompted President Theodore Roosevelt to establish Mount Olympus National Monument on March

Club mosses and other mosses cover this vine maple in the Hoh Rain Forest. Mosses are epiphytes, or plants that live upon other plants. They do not hurt the maples and can actually provide a number of benefits to the host trees, including aiding the retention of moisture.

3, 1909. The monument protected 600,000 acres in the heart of the Olympics and served as a refuge for endangered Roosevelt elk. The monument didn't include the heavily forested land along the Hoh, Queets, Quinault, and Bogachiel Rivers, however.

During World War I, President Woodrow Wilson reduced the size of National Monument by half to enable the government to harvest the Sitka spruce needed to build planes for the war effort. Twenty years later, in 1937, President Franklin Roosevelt visited the peninsula to determine the boundaries for Olympic National Park, established by Congress in 1938. The new park protected nearly 1,000 square miles of the Olympic Mountain Range. Two years later, another 300 square miles were added to the park.

In 1953, President Harry Truman added the forty-mile-long, seventy-five-square-mile strip of land between the Quinault and the Ozette Indian Reservations. The government expanded the park yet again in 1976 to include Shi Shi Beach, Point of Arches, Heart of the Hills Parkway, and the Queets watershed. Since then, the park has grown to include the intertidal zones, the offshore islands called Quillayute Needles, Flattery Rocks National Wildlife Refuge, Lake Ozette, and the Ozette River. In 1988, the government designated Olympic National Park as a federally protected wilderness area, shielding 95 percent of its land from future development. The Olympic Coast National Marine Sanctuary was created in 1994 to protect the shoreline, coastal waters, and coastal inlands.

Wild rhododendrons flourish on Mount Walker. Rhododendrons are Washington's state flower.

The Best of the Peninsula

In such a spectacular place with so many stunning sights to see, it's difficult to know where to begin. Even after thirty-two years of visiting and photographing the peninsula, there are certain sights that draw me back time and time again. I've included descriptions of those outstanding places here. As you explore the peninsula and the park yourself, I have no doubt that you'll discover your own favorite sights to add to the list.

Third Beach at La Push

From the trailhead just off of State Route 110 near the fishing village of La Push, the one-and-a-half-mile hike to Third Beach cuts through lush forest. A large line of sun-bleached drift logs marks the high tide line, and hikers must scramble over the logs to reach the beach. Vast, open Third Beach is heavy with the sound of pounding surf and the salty scent of the sea. The sandy expanse is scattered with bull kelp, rocks, and small tide pools—tiny worlds full of life in and of themselves. Bald eagles, spotted sandpipers, black oystercatchers, western and glaucous-winged gulls, and, my favorite bird, the horned puffin fly overhead and nest in the sea cliffs. Raccoons and ravens frequent the trail to and from the beach. The best time to visit Third Beach or any of the other wilderness beaches is on a day when low tide occurs around sunset. The sunsets from this beach are unforgettable. Remember to bring a good flashlight if you plan to return to your car after dark.

Hurricane Hill Hike

The trailhead for the Hurricane Hill Hike is located at the very end of the Hurricane Ridge Road, past the visitors center. Plan to hike this trail very early in the morning when there are fewer bugs, less wind, cooler temperatures, fewer hikers, more wildlife, and better light for shooting pictures. The 1.4-mile hike to the top of Hurricane Hill begins as a paved nature trail with great views of the Bailey Range.

From this vantage point, the Bailey Range appears to contain the tallest mountains in the Olympics, but that is not the case. Over the top of the Bailey Range, Mount Olympus is slightly visible. The west peak of Mount Olympus is the tallest mountain in the Olympics at 7,965 feet, and the middle peak, measuring 7,930 feet, is the second tallest.

If you continue up the trail, an Olympic marmot, a Columbia black-tailed deer, or an Olympic chipmunk may run across the path. The summit, at an altitude of 5,757 feet, is 600 feet higher than the trailhead, and on a clear day you can see forever. The entire Strait of Juan de Fuca; Port Angeles; Sequim; Dungeness Spit; Ediz Hook; Victoria and Vancouver Island, British Columbia; the Bailey Range; Mount Olympus; and the San Juan Islands are all within view.

Mount Walker Spur Road

Fifty-three miles east of Quilcene on U.S. Highway 101 is Mount Walker Spur Road. Travel to the end of Mount Walker Road for a view of Hood Canal that is second to none. In May, when the rhododendrons are in bloom (check on the time of bloom locally, as it changes from year to year), the drive to Mount Walker is stunning and fragrant.

Cape Flattery Hike

The trailhead for the Cape Flattery Trail is 8.5 miles on dirt roads from the town of Neah Bay. Before setting out on your hike, be sure to obtain a recreation permit in Neah Bay from the Makah Tribe.

From the trailhead, walk the .75 miles down the path to the lookout, perched on a cliff 200 feet above the water, for fine views of Tatoosh Island and Cape Flattery Lighthouse. The lighthouse has marked the entrance to the Strait of Juan de Fuca since 1857. Huge waves, turbulent currents, and rocky outcroppings make a good habitat for the thousands of birds that call Cape Flattery and Tatoosh Island home. Sometimes, sea lions, orcas, gray whales, and bald eagles can be seen from this vantage point.

Gray whales and humpback whales, such as the one pictured here, can be seen off the Olympic coast and in the Strait of Juan de Fuca. Gray whales pass the coast in the spring when migrating to Alaska and in the fall when returning to Mexico to calve.

The Northeast

Previous page:
The Hood Canal Floating Bridge, one of the world's few floating bridges to span a saltwater tidal basin, opened for traffic in 1961. In February 1979, the west half of the bridge sank during a storm. The bridge was rebuilt and opened to traffic in October 1982. On peak summer traffic days, as many as 20,000 vehicles use the bridge.

The gravesite of Chief Sealth sits on a hill overlooking Agate Pass and Port Madison Bay. Each August, the Suquamish tribe hosts a festival paying homage to this great Native American. Chief Sealth, the legendary leader of the Puget Sound Indians, was known for sustaining a friendly relationship with European settlers in the area. It was Chief Sealth who met and befriended Dr. David S. Maynard, the man credited with founding the city of Seattle, in Olympia, Washington, in 1850. Chief Sealth told Dr. Maynard of a much better place to build a settlement to the north, a place with a good natural harbor. Under the guidance of Chief Sealth, Maynard traveled by boat up Puget Sound to where the city of Seattle now stands.

Today, Chief Sealth's gravesite is a popular destination and jumping off point for tourists visiting the Olympic Peninsula. Located on the Kitsap Peninsula, not far from the Agate Pass Bridge and the small town of Suquamish, the site is just a short ferry ride from Seattle.

The Kitsap Peninsula

The Kitsap Peninsula, the finger of land that extends between Puget Sound and Hood Canal, is considered part of the Olympic Peninsula. Country roads wind through the peninsula's second-growth forests, connecting farmland with small towns.

Bremerton, located in the middle of the peninsula, is a quintessential Navy town. Puget Sound Naval Shipyard and the "mothball fleet" have kept the town busy since 1877, when Ambrose Wyckoff argued in favor of building the state's first naval station there.

North of Bremerton at the very tip of the Kitsap Peninsula is Point-No-Point Lighthouse, the oldest lighthouse on Puget Sound. Located near the town of Hansville, the light marks the end of Admiralty Inlet and the beginning of Puget Sound. Point-No-Point Light has been in continuous service since January 1, 1880.

Less than ten miles south of Hansville is Port Gamble, a once-bustling logging town that the Pope and Talbot Company built to house its employees in 1853. At one time, Pope and Talbot's Port Gamble Mill was the oldest continuously operating sawmill in North America. After closing in 1995, the mill was dismantled and replaced by a much smaller log chipping plant with fewer employees.

To visit Port Gamble is to step back in time. The original New England Victorian-style homes still stand and have been preserved, along with the town's general store and stately church. The historical museum, located above the town's general store, encourages a walk around the town.

The Gateway to the Olympic Peninsula

The Hood Canal Floating Bridge, officially known as the William A. Bugge Bridge, carries motorists from the Kitsap Peninsula to the Olympic Peninsula. Often referred to as the "Gateway to the Olympic Peninsula," the Hood Canal Floating Bridge is one of four permanent floating bridges in the world, all of which are located in the state of Washington. Across Hood Canal from Hansville is Port Ludlow, where the Olympic Peninsula's first sawmill was constructed in 1852. During the next ten years, several other sawmills were built on the peninsula, including ones at Discovery Bay, Chimacum Creek, and Port Gamble. The new sawmills attracted men in search of work to the area. Many of these men brought their families and settled permanently in the towns. This was the first of many logging booms to sweep the peninsula.

The grave of Chief Sealth, pictured here, is located on Agate Pass, near Old Man House State Park on the Kitsap Peninsula. The town of Suquamish is located near the grave. Sealth was a "tyee," or chief, of the Duwamish and Suquamish tribes on Puget Sound.

Chief Sealth, and his father before him, were noble friends of the whites and eager to help them in any manner. Catholic missionaries converted Sealth in the 1830s. He was the first signer of the Port Elliott Treaty in 1855, by which the Washington tribes were given a reservation. The City of Seattle is named after this great chief.

Today, all of the mills have closed and most of the workers have left the area. Port Ludlow has become a retirement community and a resort town, Discovery Bay is all but abandoned, and Chimacum Creek is an agricultural center.

The Quilcene/Brinnon area, located southwest of the Hood Canal Floating Bridge, is famous for its logging traditions. Now Quilcene and Brinnon are the oyster, shrimp, and clam capitals of the peninsula. Brinnon holds an annual Shrimpfest the first weekend of shrimp season (third weekend in May), and shrimpers come from all over the Northwest to fish the canal's rich waters. Shrimpfest often coincides with the peak rhododendron season, and Whitney Gardens in Brinnon features breathtaking displays of the state flower. The Dosewallips River, Rocky Brook Falls, and Falls View State Park are all within a half-hour drive of Quilcene and Brinnon.

The Gem of the Northeast

Twenty-four miles north of the Hood Canal Floating Bridge, on the northwestern tip of the Olympic Peninsula, is picturesque Port Townsend. Settled in the 1850s, Port Townsend was the main port of entry into Puget Sound. The seaport prospered in the 1880s, and it was during this boom time that many of the town's beautiful Victorian buildings were constructed. In 1890, however, the Northern Pacific Railroad chose Seattle as the terminus instead of Port Townsend, and the town went bust. But the handsome three-story brick buildings remained, serving as a great legacy from the past.

Today, tourism is Port Townsend's main industry. Historic Water Street features art galleries, antique shops, gift stores, and restaurants. Most of the town's elaborate Victorian houses, located on the hill overlooking the city and Port Townsend Harbor, have been restored and converted into bed-and-breakfast inns.

Just off the coast of Port Townsend is Marrowstone Island, home of Fort Flagler State Park. Fort Flagler was built in the late 1890s to protect the settlements in the Puget Sound region. Today, the fort is part of a large marine camping park, surrounded on three sides by saltwater beaches. Visitors may explore the military museum, which includes relics of the old fort and an interactive display. Many of the fort's historic buildings remain, including gun emplacements, and guided tours of the fort are offered during the summer months.

The Walker-Ames House, located in Port Gamble, was built in 1887 for William Walker, a master mechanic at the Port Gamble Pope and Talbot Mill. The style and size of the home is indicative of the wealth and prosperity of the mill, which was the largest lumber mill on Puget Sound. The house was built close to the mill so Walker would be nearby in case of an emergency. Ames was the mill resident manager from 1883 to 1914, then general manager until 1931. Walker lived here with his wife Emma, daughter Maude, and son-in-law Edwin Ames.

The clock tower on Port Townsend's Jefferson County Courthouse was built with 4 million bricks shipped here from St. Louis in 1890. The courthouse has stood the test of time. The 10-foot-square and 124-foot-high clock tower is a prominent landmark in Port Townsend.

Built in 1889, the James and Hastings Building was one of four buildings bearing the name of Loren B. Hastings, who died eight years before it was completed. Originally, Smith and Ellis Dry Goods occupied the ground floor. The company sold clothing, footwear, and hardware items such as tinware and other household goods. The upper floors of the James and Hastings Building housed small offices and apartments.

When it was completed the Hastings Building was said to be the most elegant building in Port Townsend. At the whopping cost of $25,000, it was the most expensive commercial building as well.

Above:

This brilliant spiral staircase greets visitors who enter the Ann Starrett Mansion lobby. The staircase is well known among architecture buffs because the large structure stands entirely unsupported.

Facing page:

The George E. Starrett House has been called the best example of Port Townsend's Victorian architecture. The home was designed and built in 1889 by George Starrett, who was the major residential builder in Port Townsend at the time. The house has been pictured in *National Geographic, Sunset,* and other publications. It is now a very successful bed and breakfast operated under the name Ann Starrett Mansion.

Above:
This tidy wooden boat is moored at Point Hudson Marina in Port Townsend Harbor.

Left:
Boats at rest in Point Hudson Marina and Resort in Port Townsend. Point Hudson Marina, is located just north of Port Townsend at the entrance to Admiralty Inlet. It is the home of the Wooden Boat Festival, which is held each year during the weekend after Labor Day.

Above:

Twigs, a small shop in Port Townsend, is just one of the many unique establishments that feature the best antiques and handmade treasures crafted by local peninsula artisans. The town boasts antique malls, quaint bookshops, consignment shops, and music stores. Year-round farmer's markets and craft shows are held in both Uptown and downtown Port Townsend. The Uptown neighborhood itself is a nationally registered historic district.

Facing page:

The Point Wilson Lighthouse marks the easternmost portion of the Strait of Juan de Fuca and the beginning of Admiralty Inlet. Captain George Vancouver named the point in honor of his friend Captain George Wilson of the British Navy. The first lighthouse at this site was completed in 1879, and the present lighthouse and keeper's quarters were built in 1914. The lighthouse and Coast Guard station are now part of Fort Worden State Park.

The ferry "Klickitat" arrives at Keystone Ferry Terminal at Admiralty Head on Whidbey Island. The "Klickitat" and another ferry, the "Quinault," make more than 15 round trips per day carrying as many as 75 cars and more than 600 passengers per trip. The Keystone/Port Townsend run is one of the six ferry routes carrying passengers, cars, and commercial vehicles to the peninsula.

Above:
The remains of the Discovery Bay sawmill still stand on lower Discovery Bay. San Francisco entrepreneur S. B. Mastick and his partner started the mill around 1860. At its peak, the mill employed 300 people. But the mill had to be closed in about 1900 when it ran out of land to log.

Facing page:
This old fishing boat is anchored in Discovery Bay.

A gillnet fisherman sets a net near Port Townsend on Hood Canal. Gillnet fishing has a long history on the Olympic Peninsula. It is the oldest form of industrial salmon fishing on the Northwest coast. Native American fishermen were the first to use gill nets. Gillnetters string a net out in a water source, such as an estuary or an ocean, to block the salmon's path. Gill nets can also be used farther upstream in large rivers like the Quinault, Queets, and Hoh. The salmon swim into the net but are unable to go through because the mesh is too small. When the fish try to back out of the net, their gill covers get snagged in the netting. This method of catching fish is very effective because the nets can be made to select fish by both size and species in any given run. Although the equipment has become more modern, the principles behind gillnetting have not changed over the years.

Located in the town of Union on the lower end of Hood Canal, the Dalby Water Wheel was one of the first hydroelectric plants in western Washington.

Above:

The Dungeness crab, famous for its sweet flavor, heavy claws, and the large pieces of meat beneath its carapace, is the staple of Pacific coast recreational and commercial crabbers. The crabs are named after the sand flats and eel grass beds inside Dungeness Spit, home to one of the region's first commercial crab fisheries. Dungeness crabs can grow as large as ten inches across the carapace, but usually average six or seven inches.

Left:

On April 30, 1792, Captain George Vancouver named Dungeness Bay which is formed by the Dungeness Spit. At seven miles long, the Dungeness Spit is the longest natural spit in the world. This fragile piece of land, formed by the interaction between the waters of the Pacific Ocean and the Dungeness River, narrows to as little as fifty feet wide in places and is sometimes breached by high tides and rough seas. The original lighthouse at the end of the Dungeness Spit was built in 1857 as part of a four-lighthouse chain along the strait.

Above:
Pass Lake in Deception Pass State Park on Whidbey Island is one of best fishing lakes in western Washington. The lake is restricted to fly fishing only.

Facing page:
A visitor takes in the scenery on Bowman Bay landing, part of Deception Pass State Park. A narrow band of water separates the north end of Whidbey Island from the mainland. The Deception Pass Bridge is a well-known feat of engineering that joins Fidalgo Island to Whidbey Island.

The Northern Shore

The Strait of Juan de Fuca defines the northern shore of the Olympic Peninsula. The eighty miles of coastline along the strait varies from jagged, rocky cliffs to sandy, crescent-shaped beaches. At any given point, the strait is twelve to sixteen miles wide. On a clear day, the Canadian city of Victoria, British Columbia, on Vancouver Island is easily visible from the shore.

Fishing, both commercial and for sport, is big business along the strait. Clallam Bay and Sekui are world famous for salmon, halibut, lingcod, and red snapper. Though the salmon runs are nothing compared to what they were seventy years ago, most years they are still some of the largest around.

Sequim

Thirty-one miles west of Port Townsend on U.S. Highway 101, the town of Sequim is nestled between the Olympic Mountains and the sunny side of the Strait of Juan de Fuca in the Dungeness Valley. Sequim is like no other place in the world. Located in the rain shadow of the Olympic Mountains, Sequim, which means "quiet water" in the Clallam Indian language, enjoys moderate weather with only sixteen inches of rainfall on average each year. The seven-mile-long Dungeness Spit near Sequim is the world's largest natural sand spit.

Farmers who work the small farms in the area, most of which raise potatoes, wheat, oats, and peas, need to irrigate because of the scant rainfall. The community holds a week-long irrigation festival in early May to celebrate the opening of the floodgates of the flumes, which were built in 1896 to carry water from the Dungeness River to the fields on the Sequim Prairie. The celebration is Washington's oldest annual festival.

Port Angeles

Port Angeles, a deep-water seaport on the strait, is the largest city on the northern Olympic Peninsula. Ediz Hook, a three-mile-long strip of land that extends east from the city, creates a protected harbor for ocean going freighters, fishing vessels, and ferries. Ships traveling to and from Seattle, Tacoma, Olympia, Bellingham, and Vancouver frequently travel the strait, and Port Angeles is their main stop along the route.

The history of the Olympic Peninsula is closely tied to the timber industry, and Port Angeles is no exception. It was the development of the pulp and paper mills that put Port Angeles on the map. To this day, wood harvest and processing businesses are the city's heartbeat. In the early years, logging companies all over the peninsula harvested only the easy-to-reach waterfront stands of trees. Peninsula and Puget Sound timberlands produced five times more timber per acre than eastern for-

Previous pages:
Located on the Strait of Juan de Fuca at the foot of the Olympic Mountains, Port Angeles is the gateway to Olympic National Park and the Pacific coast beaches. In this view from Ediz Hook across rafts of Douglas fir in Port Angeles Harbor, western Port Angeles and Olympic National Park's Hurricane Ridge are in the background. The rafts will be towed into Puget Sound where the logs will be cut into dimensioned lumber.

Facing page:
A sailing ship bobs on the sixteen-mile-wide Strait of Juan de Fuca near Port Angeles.

ests, which were the primary source of lumber in the United States until the Civil War.

Now, the timber industry has fallen on hard times. The controversy over the northern spotted owl habitat, the Wilderness Act of 1964, set-asides, and many other laws and regulations have drastically reduced the amount of land available for harvesting. This, in turn, has greatly reduced the amount of wood available for milling into lumber and the number of raw logs passing through the port for shipment to Japan and Canada.

Sekui and Callam Bay

Farther west along the coast are the twin cities of Sekui and Clallam Bay. The town center of Sekui, a Clallam Indian word meaning "calm water," is only 2.4 miles from Clallam Bay. At one time, the two towns were called West Clallam Bay and East Clallam Bay, but in 1907, West Clallam Bay changed its name to Sekui to distinguish itself from its neighbor to the east.

In 1870, a Seattle company moved its operations to Clallam Bay to can salmon at the source rather than transport the fish all the way back into Puget Sound. In 1887, a tanbark plant opened in the area. Tanbark, a solution made from the bark of hemlock trees, was used to cure leather. Large crews of men cut virgin stands of hemlock, peeled the bark from the trees, and left the wood to rot. At the time, hemlock was considered worthless for lumber.

By the mid 1890s, the cost of producing tanbark had risen and the introduction of new tanning methods changed the commercial tanning industry forever. When the market collapsed, the Clallam Bay plant closed and most of the workers went to work in the fishing or canning industries.

Large-scale logging in the area began in 1907 and subsided in the 1970s. Lumber companies harvested 650,000 board feet of Douglas fir on a single acre along the Hoko River. By 1985, both the old-growth forest and the salmon in commercial quantities were depleted. The resources had lasted less than a century. Today, Sekui and Clallam Bay are famous for fine sport salmon fishing, bird watching, coastal hiking, beach combing, whale watching, wildlife cruises, and sea kayaking.

Facing page:

The *Red Baron* rests in Boat Heaven Boat Harbor in Port Angeles Harbor.

Left:

Pilings from an old Port Angeles cannery are decorated with metal bird sculptures.

From the overlook just before Snow Creek Resort on Highway 112, the road between Sekui and Neah Bay, you can see Sail Rock and Seal Rock, which are located near the western extremity of the Strait of Juan de Fuca. Seal Rock is pictured here. These rocks provide essential offshore nesting spots that make the Cape Flattery area so important to the bird world. The unique geology of Seal Rock and of other rocks in the area, called sea stacks, make prime nesting sites for seabirds.

According to legend, the logging business on the peninsula got its start when a ship sailed from San Francisco to Puget Sound to get a load of ice. Of course, there was no ice for the ship to load. The ship's captain decided that he would not return with an empty ship so he ordered his crew to fill the ship with logs, which were readily available along the Strait of Juan de Fuca. A vessel could anchor near shore almost anywhere and easily fill the ship with large, straight trees. A new industry, the logging industry, had been born.

These log rafts at Port Angeles Harbor are being dismantled and loaded on barges for shipment to mills on lower Puget Sound. In recent years the timber harvesting has been restricted due to ecological concerns and international trade considerations. The logging industry on the peninsula has been hit hard.

Logging trucks are required to stop at scaling stations to compute stumpage and hauling fees and to measure the amount of timber being harvested. This station is along U.S. Highway 101.

Rafting large groups of logs is a very economical way to transport them to market or to mills. These logging rafts float in Port Angeles Harbor.

The summer sun sets dramatically behind Port Angeles Harbor, Ediz Hook, City Pier, and the Strait of Juan de Fuca. Passengers on the Chinook ferry, which carries vehicles and passengers to the city of Victoria on Vancouver Island, British Columbia, have the best view around.

This giant mushroom looms alongside U.S. Highway 101 outside of Port Angeles. It's been carved out of one big cedar stump.

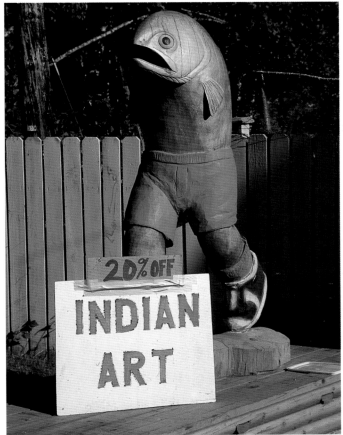

20% OFF

INDIAN ART

The abundance of trees on the peninsula makes carving a popular craft among native peoples. This carving stands outside a shop near Sekui.

Canada geese float on
Aldwell Lake.

Above:
Fall brings brightly colored leaves to the verdant, moss-covered
Elwha Valley.

Facing page:
Aldwell Lake is formed by the Lower Elwha Dam, which is scheduled
to be removed in 2003. Built in the early 1900s, the Lower Elwha
Dam and Glines Canyon Dam blocked access of salmon and steelhead to more than seventy miles of stream habitat.
The Elwha watershed is the largest in Olympic National Park. It
contains some of the best old-growth Douglas fir forests in the park,
with many trees measuring eight feet or larger in diameter.

Above:

Young beachcombers peruse a beach near Sekui at low tide. Cobble beaches are very common along the strait and in protected coves on the Pacific coast. The native littleneck and butter clams and the introduced Japanese littleneck are relatively easy to find along the strait.

Facing page:

During sunset, the view from the northern coast across the Strait of Juan de Fuca to Vancouver Island, British Columbia, can be spectacular. Varied wildlife, including orcas, humpback and California gray whales, seals, sea otters, and bald eagles, infuse the shoreline of the strait. Farther inland, deer roam through the deep forests of Sitka spruce and western red cedar. Lonely stretches of cobbled beaches, towering headlands, river mouths, coastal cliffs, and narrow beaches—features typical of the strait—mark the shoreline.

The Northwest

The view from the third lookout platform at the end of the Cape Trail on Cape Flattery is like peering over the edge of the world. From this 200-foot-high perch on a rocky cliff at the westernmost point of the lower forty-eight states, the vast, blue Pacific Ocean stretches to the distant horizon. Below the platform, Hole-in-the-Wall and Lookthrough-Rock Arch punctuate the cliff face. A half-mile off shore, Tatoosh Island, the most rugged piece of land you can possibly imagine, is clearly visible. Three sides of the island are unapproachable, guarded by dangerous shoals and rocks that extend well beyond the island's very steep cliffs. A small beach on the east side of Tatoosh might accommodate the landing of a small boat in calm seas. The Cape Flattery Lighthouse, built in 1857, stands on one of the island's only flat spots.

Wildlife abounds on Cape Flattery. Gray whales, humpback whales, and orcas are regularly seen from this viewpoint and from the other two lookout platforms along the Cape Trail. Many smaller marine mammals, such as harbor seals, sea lions, Dall's porpoise, harbor porpoise, and sea otters live in the area, too. Shorebirds, such as cormorants, ducks, black oystercatchers, glaucous-winged gulls, western gulls, common murre, marbled murrelet, horned puffins, and even bald eagles make themselves at home among the rocks.

Neah Bay

The .75-mile hike back to the trailhead cuts through a very dense growth of forest. The town of Neah Bay, the most northwesterly community in the United States, is 8.5 miles east, on dirt roads. Neah Bay is one of the best places in the country to fish for salmon, and commercial fishing is one of the mainstays of the community. Whale-watching, tide-pooling, hiking, and camping are also very popular here.

Located on the Makah Indian Reservation, Neah Bay is the ancestral home of the Makah people. The Makahs call themselves "Kwih-dich-chuh-ahtx" or "people who live by the rocks and seagulls." The name "Makah," which means "generous with food" in the Salish language, was given to the band by their neighboring tribes.

The Makahs are the only Native American tribe whose right to hunt whales is guaranteed by treaty. Whaling has been a tradition of the Makah for more than 2,000 years. The tribe was forced to stop hunting in the 1920s due to the scarcity of gray whales. The tribe's decision to begin hunting whales again was a very controversial one, even within the Makah tribe.

Under the treaty signed in 1855, the United States granted the Makahs the right to engage in whaling. Today, the terms of the Makah Whale Management Plan dictate how many whales the tribe may hunt each year.

The Makah Cultural Research Center, which opened in Neah Bay

On December 16, 1929, the 240-foot *Skagway* was en route from San Francisco to Seattle with a crew of twenty-six. Her cargo caught fire in a heavy gale as she rounded Tatoosh Island. The captain attempted to seek the shelter of the island to prevent the high winds from fanning the flames. The ship reached the backside of the island but grounded more than once and finally took on a heavy list. The captain deliberately ran her aground again to prevent her from sinking. The crew was able to escape from the ship before it was torn apart by the sea.

in 1979, has one of the finest collections of Native American artifacts in the Northwest. Exhibits feature full-scale replicas of cedar longhouses and canoes made for whaling, sealing, and fishing. The museum houses the largest archaeological collection held by any tribe in the United States. Many of the best artifacts recovered from the Ozette Village archaeological site and from a dig at the ancient fishing village located at the mouth of the Hoko River are on display here.

Shi Shi Beach and Point of Arches

Southwest of Neah Bay is Mukkaw Bay, the trailhead for the four-mile hike to Shi Shi Beach. Shi Shi Beach, the northernmost beach on the coastal strip of Olympic National Park, is the most spectacular beach in the park. The crescent-shaped strip of sandy beach stretches for two miles along the shore, anchored by the Makah Indian Reservation in the north and by Point of Arches, the most impressive headland on the Olympic Coast, in the south. Rugged sea stacks, jagged rocks, and delicate arches line the shore. Shi Shi Beach and Point of Arches became part of the park in 1976.

Farther down the coast, is Ozette Village. In 1970 tidal erosion revealed this ancient whaling village, parts of which had been covered by a mudslide hundreds of years ago. The site, one of the most significant archaeological discoveries made in North America, is not open to the public, so a visit to the Makah Cultural Research Center in Neah Bay is worthwhile.

Bottom left:

Ozette Village, located near Cape Alava, is an archaeological site that was buried by a mudslide 500 years ago. More than 50,000 objects were recovered and are on display in the Makah Cultural Research Center in Neah Bay. Nearby is Wedding Rocks, where 500-year-old petroglyphs can be found. This one is of an orca.

Bottom right:

Heart-shaped beadruby grows near the Salt Creek area, which is located along the northern edge of the Strait of Juan de Fuca.

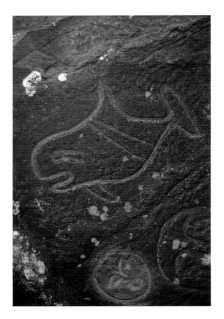

A commercial salmon troller unloads its catch in the picturesque harbor of Neah Bay, located at the mouth of the Strait of Juan de Fuca. The area around Neah Bay is considered to be some of the best commercial and sport fishing waters in the contiguous United States. Several types of salmon—including Chinook, silver (also called Coho), Sockeye, chum, and pink—are caught in the Strait of Juan de Fuca.

Above:

Children perform dances at the Makah Days annual celebration. Held during the last weekend in August, the festivities commemorate the raising of the U.S. flag at Neah Bay on August 26, 1913, and the granting of U.S. citizenship to Native Americans on June 1, 1924. Activities during Makah Days include dugout canoe races, bone games (a form of Native gambling), Native American dances, a baseball tournament, and a salmon bake.

Right:

For the Makah Days salmon bake, the Makah cook butterfly salmon on cedar stakes and smoke-cook the fillets over alder fires.

Facing page:

These fishing boats are tied up to Neah Bay pier within the Makah Indian Reservation in the northwest corner of the Olympic Peninsula.

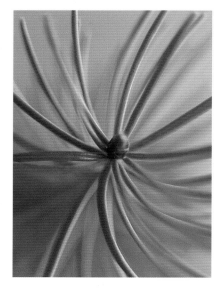

Right:

Next to the California redwood, the Douglas fir is the largest tree in the western United States. The world's largest Douglas fir tree, measuring 14 feet 6 inches in diameter, is located 2.5 miles beyond the end of the Queets Rain Forest Road. It is 225 feet tall.

Above:

Tree farms, such as this one located on Highway 101, are in the business of planting, growing, tending, and selling forest crops.

Right:

Douglas fir is the most common tree on the Olympic Peninsula. The tree in this photo is believed to be more than 750 years old. The trees make ideal lumber because the trunks are thick, straight, and tough fibered.

The Olympic Peninsula has twelve species of owls, including the great horned owl pictured here, but only the western screech owl, the saw-whet owl, and the northern pygmy owl are common. The northern spotted owl's designation ten years ago as a threatened species under the U.S. Endangered Species Act lead to a fiery dispute between environmentalists and loggers. The environmentalists say that the owls are dependent on the old-growth forests for their habitat. Timber companies favor old-growth forests because they can harvest larger amounts of wood from each old-growth tree. The federal government sharply restricts logging within a 2,000-acre area surrounding a known spotted owl nest and requires that at least 500 acres of the largest trees within that zone be left uncut. The government also prohibits logging within a 70-acre area immediately surrounding a nest.

Above:

Cape Flattery Lighthouse perches high on a Tatoosh Island cliff. The treacherous rocky outcroppings that surround the island justify the need for a lighthouse in the area.

Facing page:

This time-worn, storm-damaged boat is tied to a pier in Neah Bay on the Makah Reservation.

The corn lily plant thrives in the shady, moist environment of the Olympic Peninsula rain forest.

Above:
Foxglove flourishes throughout the Olympic Peninsula. During the summertime, the peninsula is alive with the color of foxglove and fireweed.

Facing page:
This boardwalk marks the beginning of the 3.3-mile Cape Alava Trail. Cape Alava is the site of an ancient Makah village that was partially buried in a mudslide more than 500 years ago. Continue one mile farther down the beach to see the 300-year-old petroglyphs at Wedding Rocks.

Olympic National Park

In the depths of the Hoh Rain Forest, towering Sitka spruce, western hemlock, Douglas fir, and red cedar prevent rays of sunshine from ever touching the forest floor. But lack of sunlight doesn't prevent plants from taking root in any space available. Liverworts, oxalis, maidenhair ferns, sword ferns, herbs, grasses, shrubs, and seedlings flourish between the trees. In this rich environment, the trees that fall to the forest floor due to old age, disease, or heavy winds begin to break down and rot on the moist earth. These old trees, called nurse logs, provide the perfect growing medium for millions of tiny seedlings. Epiphytes, such as vibrant green mosses, blanket rotting nurse logs on the forest floor and hang from the limbs overhead. Licorice ferns sprout from trunks and branches of the giant trees while lichens and seedlings cling to the bark.

Roosevelt elk, black-tailed deer, cougars, black bears, river otters, and squirrels search for food on the lush, green forest floor. The air hums with the sound of insects and birds of all kinds, including varied thrush, gray jay, and winter wren, which soar among the branches and towering trees.

Rain Forest

The Hoh Rain Forest is one of four temperate rain forest valleys that span the western edge of the Olympic Range in Olympic National Park. Together, the Hoh, Queets, Quinault, and Bogachiel rain forest valleys make up what is thought to be the best remaining example of a Northwest rain forest.

Moisture-laden clouds, driven across the peninsula by prevailing winds off the Pacific Ocean, supply the rain needed to nourish this amazing ecosystem. The Hoh Rain Forest receives anywhere from 130 inches to 145 inches of rain each year. The fog that rolls in from the coast also contributes to the moisture content of the forests, accumulating on the leaves of trees and eventually falling to the ground as rain. Thirty inches of the total rainfall that the Hoh Rain Forest receives each year is in the form of fog condensation.

Previous pages:
The peaks of the Bailey Range provide a crisp backdrop to the glacially carved valley.

Facing page:
A palette of green dominates the Hall of Mosses Trail in the Hoh Rain Forest of Olympic National Park. The park's boundaries include unique wilderness beaches and rugged snow-covered mountains, but its most spectacular features are the temperate rain forests, home to the most magnificent collection of giant conifers in the world. The area's temperate climate and abundant rain stimulates forest growth. And the Olympic Peninsula's location, halfway between the equator and the North Pole, means that it receives optimum sunshine during the growing season. Last but not least, the rich volcanic and sedimentary soils that make up the Olympic Mountains are perfect nourishment for forests. The temperate rain forest growth rate per acre here is better than any other ecosystem in the world, including tropical rain forests.

A Columbia black-tailed deer grazes at Hurricane Ridge. Male blacktails have branched antlers. Their coats are reddish in summer and grayish brown in winter. The bucks can weigh as much as 250 pounds, while does weigh much less. Many blacktails live throughout the park.

Mountains

On the craggy Olympic Mountains that dominate the heart of the park, precipitation falls as snow, feeding more than sixty glaciers. Run-off from these glaciers supplies water to the peninsula's thirteen major river systems, including the Dosewallips, Dungeness, Elwha, Hoh, Queets, and Quinault. In turn, these glaciers continue to chip away at the mountains.

Mount Olympus, the tallest peak in the Olympic Range, rises to a summit of 7,965 feet. Although the elevation is not high by Cascade or Rocky Mountain standards, the overall rate of climb in the Olympics is greater than the rise of the Grand Tetons above Jackson Hole, Wyoming. Thirty-seven other peaks within the range tower more than 7,000 feet in elevation.

Hurricane Ridge, located on the northeastern edge of the Olympics, offers a great view of the tallest mountains to the southwest. At an altitude of about 5,000 feet, alpine meadows stretch across the ridge. In the summertime, the Olympic magenta painted cup, Piper's bellflower, Flett's violet, and other wildflowers bloom among the grasses and shrubs. Columbia black-tailed deer and Olympic marmots scour the grassy hillsides, looking for food.

Coast

Watching a sunset from Third Beach, Rialto Beach, Ruby Beach, or any of the other wilderness beaches at low tide is an experience not to be missed. Sea stacks, towering sandstone islands formed over thousands of years by the action of the wind and surf, dot the coast. Sun-bleached driftwood, remnants of fallen Sitka spruce and other rain forest giants that have washed down one of the peninsula's many rivers, are scattered across these beaches.

Off the rugged Washington coast, more than 3,300 square miles of ocean waters make up the Olympic Coast National Marine Sanctuary. Sanctuary waters extend an average of 35 miles offshore and span 135 miles north to south, from Cape Flattery to the Copalis River.

The Olympic Coast National Marine Sanctuary is full of biological superlatives. More species of whales, dolphins, and porpoises spend time in these waters and more kinds of kelp are found here than anywhere else in the world. Twenty-nine species of marine mammals—including the harbor seal, harbor porpoise, Pacific white-sided dolphin, Risso's dolphin, humpback whale, and California gray whale—breed, rest within, or migrate through the sanctuary waters. The sanctuary contains some of the largest colonies of seabirds, such as murres and tufted puffins, in the contiguous United States. The sanctuary coastline is home to one of the largest populations of bald eagles in the lower forty-eight states. During

annual migrations, the total population of seabirds, waterfowl, and shore-birds along the coast may exceed one million animals. Seven species of Pacific salmon, sea-run cutthroat trout, steelhead trout, albacore tuna, Pacific halibut, flounder, sole, numerous species of rockfish, Pacific cod, Pacific hake, lingcod, sablefish, thresher shark, Pacific herring, northern anchovy, jack mackerel, pollock, spiny dogfish, and sturgeon are other important components of the sanctuary ecosystem.

Early October snow covers the high country near Hurricane Hill. At higher elevations, such as Hurricane Ridge, snowfall is usually heavy, and accumulations of up to ten feet are very common.

The Future

In 1976, the United Nations made Olympic National Park a biosphere reserve. These areas represent particular biomes that still exist in as close to their original form as possible. The United Nations chose Olympic National Park because of its pristine temperate rain forests, one of only three areas like this in the world. In 1982, the park was designated a World Heritage Site, an area that exhibits extraordinary traits of either nature or culture. Olympic National Park shares this honor with more than a hundred sites, including the Galapagos Islands, Chartres Cathedral, and the Taj Mahal. With a little luck and a lot of work, these designations should help preserve and protect the park for generations to come.

Above:
The Piper's bellflower, pictured here, is one of eight species of plants found only on the Olympic Peninsula and nowhere else in the world.

Left:
By the late 1880s, only a few places in America had not been explored, and the interior of the Olympic Peninsula was one of them. The remoteness, steep approaches, and dense vegetation had discouraged most European explorers. In 1889, the Press Expedition explored the Elwha valley route.

Above:

The most revered aspect of the ancient forest is its large trees. The Olympic Peninsula is blessed with the best tree-growing climate in the world. Extraordinary amounts of rain and moderate temperatures allow long-lived species to reach more than 250 feet in height and 8 feet or larger in diameter.

Facing page:

These subalpine fir create a small "silver forest" at Hurricane Ridge. The subalpine fir on Hurricane Ridge have a very harsh existence and have a much shorter life span (200 years) than other evergreen species in the Olympic Mountains. Most species have a life span of 700 years or more. Typically, subalpine fir grow very slowly because they spend six months of the year under snow. Many of these trees are damaged by the extremely high winds that are known to pummel the ridge.

Above:

The Elwha, which drains the park's largest watershed, is ideal for whitewater rafting. At the turn of the century, seven different species of salmon and sea-run trout migrated up the river to spawn. Chinook salmon migrate in the spring, some of them once weighed more than 100 pounds.

Facing page:

Big-leaf maples, such as this one along the Elwha, thrive in the lower reaches of valley bottoms in the park. Big-leaf maples are more likely to sport epiphytes—mosses and ferns—than most other trees.

Above, top:
This bracket fungus grows on a tree trunk near the edge of the Angeles Lake Trail.

Above, bottom:
The park's many red alder trees host lichens, which give their bark a white and splotchy appearance.

This Sitka spruce stump, located on the Moments In Time Interpretive Trail near the ranger station on Lake Crescent, was cut in about 1910 with the help of a springboard. If you look closely, you can still see the notch into which the springboard rested. Springboards served as platforms for loggers as they manually sawed large trees.

Lake Crescent Lodge's "wicker cozy" sun porch invites guests to relax. The lodge, originally called Singer's Tavern, was built on Barns Point in 1915. In 1938, President Franklin Roosevelt spent the night at the tavern while on an inspection tour of the soon-to-be Olympic National Park.

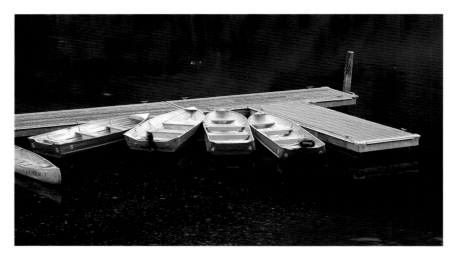

Early morning dawns on the western end of Lake Crescent at Fairholm Resort.

A lone red fishing boat skims the surface on the west end of Lake Crescent. The isolated environment of the lake led to the growth of two unique species of fish: the Beardslee rainbow trout and the Lake Crescent cutthroat trout. Both the rainbow and the cutthroat have been hybridized out of existence by the introduction of other varieties of cutthroat and rainbow trout. But, the lake is still considered a good place to fish.

Oxalis is often mistaken for shamrock. Oxalis grows just off the Marymere Falls Trail near Lake Crescent.

Above:
A rustic log bridge crosses Barns Creek just below Marymere Falls.

Facing page:
Falls Creek plunges and horsetails over a rock wall to form Marymere Falls near Lake Crescent. The falls is an easy half-mile hike from Lake Crescent Ranger Station.

An adult cougar saunters down to a small creek for a drink of water. Cougars are becoming more and more of a problem on the peninsula. As the prime forestlands are logged, cleared for farming, or subdivided for new homes and small ranchettes, the large cats must look for new territories. The number of close encounters between people and large cats has increased dramatically over the past few years.

Fall colors are a main attraction on the Quillayute Indian Reservation near La Push.

Facing page:
This small stream crosses the Sol Duc Falls Trail about .5 mile from the falls. At .9 mile each way, the trail is one of the most popular hikes in Olympic National Park. Sol Duc Falls is the largest falls in this area and the most photographed of all the waterfalls in the park. The name *Sol Duc* is a corruption of the Quillayute words meaning "magic waters." Native Americans called the mineral water that bubbles from the earth here *skukum lemenser* or "strong medicine."

Banana slugs, signature creatures of the peninsula, are very common in the rain forests of Olympic National Park. These huge specimens are so named because very often their coloring resembles a banana. The slugs have a bright yellow body with black spots. At up to six inches long, banana slugs are the second-largest species of mollusks in the world. The coloring of the banana slug varies from solid green, to pale brown, to almost white. The wily slugs are able to change their coloring slightly over time to better hide among the leaves on the rain forest floor.

Above:

The rush of water over Sol Duc Falls can be heard long before hikers reach it. Just before the trail approaches the falls, it passes the Canyon Creek shelter, built by the Civilian Conservation Corps. The shelter is well worth a visit. A one-of-a-kind structure with a cupola, it's a good place to leave your pack on a wet day while you hike a bit farther to view the falls.

Facing page:

These red alder trees grow near Sol Duc Hot Springs Resort. Red alder is often mistaken for birch because of the white-gray lichens that grow on the tree's bark. Red alder have a short life span; a fifty-year-old tree is considered quite ancient. These trees are vital to forest succession because they host nitrogen-fixing bacteria, which prepares the soil for the introduction of spruce and hemlock, trees that form the foundation of the temperate rain forests.

To step into the temperate rain forest on the west side of the Olympic Peninsula, such as this second- or third-growth stand in the Quinault Rain Forest, is to enter a world hushed and ethereal, swathed in solemn, luxuriant, stately abundance. It is a realm where mosses and ferns cling to overhead branches and seedlings carpet prostrate nurse logs. Minute soil fungi nourish conifer trees that tower 150 feet before branching out. Animals also play a part in this great ecosystem. Elk and deer browse and trample brush and small trees, allowing more sunlight into the forest.

Above:

Lake Quinault Lodge, a rustic resort hotel built in 1926, is one of many lodges built on the peninsula in the area that became Olympic National Park. The totem pole that rests against the Lodge's giant chimney is actually a rain gauge.

Right:

Skunk cabbage is one of the first plants to bloom in the spring, and many animals, including black bears, find it a nourishing meal during a time when food is sometimes scarce. This skunk cabbage grows in the Quinault Rain Forest.

The 18.1-mile Enchanted Valley Trail crosses this bridge over Graves Creek at the Graves Creek Trailhead. This hike is called the "Valley of 10,000 Waterfalls," which is said to be one of the most beautiful waterfall areas in the world.

Above:

This upper intertidal zone, located at Olympic National Park Beach Number 4, is normally flooded during high tides. The upper zone is home to acorn barnacles, mussels, turban snails, hermit crabs, and shore crabs. This is just one of many access points along U.S. Highway 101.

Left:

The action of the surf on Rialto Beach has polished these rocks smooth. The surf along the entire western edge of the Olympic Peninsula is particularly high during the fall and winter months.

Facing page:

The southernmost of the six Olympic National Park beaches is Beach Number 1, the Spruce Burl Forest. The round knobs that grow on the trees are actually tumors. Damage to the tip or the bud of a Sitka spruce causes the growth cells to divide more rapidly than normal to form this swelling or burl. Even though the burls may look menacing, they do not affect the overall tree growth.

These two small, brown-colored black bears live at the Olympic Game Farm, home to many animals native and nonnative to the Olympic Peninsula. Many of these animals have been seen in Disney films and the *Grizzly Adams* television series. Starting in the 1950s, Disney photographer Lloyd Beebe began photographing black bears, grizzly bears, bison, elk, yak, deer, peacocks, cougars, and gray wolves for the Disney farms collection.

This young Roosevelt elk bull takes an early morning stroll. Roosevelt elk are larger than the more common Rocky Mountain elk found in Yellowstone National Park and the Rocky Mountain Range. Named for the president and conservationist Theodore Roosevelt, the Roosevelt elk is a coastal variety that lives from British Columbia to Northern California.

Facing page:
The water that flows over Rocky Brook Falls continues to erode the rock and shape the landscape.

Above:
Salmon spawn in a creek near Olympia.

Left:
The Olympic Peninsula is home to seven types of salmon which includes the rainbow and cutthroat trout. These fishermen are hoping to catch a steelhead on the Dosewallips River.

The Western Coast

From Cape Flattery south to Ocean Shores, a distance of some sixty miles, stretches the longest span of undeveloped beach between Canada and Mexico. Much of the northern section of this coastline, from just south of Neah Bay to just north of Queets, is under the protection of Olympic National Park and three Indian reservations.

The wild and rugged Olympic coast is particularly beautiful. Over thousands of years, wind, rain, and seawater have carved arches and glorious sea stacks from islets of sandstone. The tide continuously picks up fractured rock and sand and redeposits them on countless beaches and coves, changing the landscape many times over.

La Push

The name La Push, derived from *la bouche,* the French word for "mouth," refers to the mouth of the Quillayute River, where the town is located. La Push has been the home of the Quillayute tribe for the past 2,000 years.

La Push is famous for some of the most spectacular and rugged scenery in the coastal section of Olympic National Park. Third Beach, Second Beach, and Rialto Beach—some of the best wilderness beaches in the park—are all within a few miles of La Push. Third beach is one of the most beautiful places in the state of Washington. Sun-bleached driftwood periodically washes up on the fine-grained sand and pebble beach before coming to rest at the beach's high tide line. Just off shore stands a wonderful sea stack with a lone evergreen tree sprouting from the top.

Forks

Almost directly east of La Push is Forks, the commercial center of the northwestern peninsula. If Sequim is known for sunshine, then Forks is known for rain, receiving more than any other city in the United States. On average, 114 inches of rain saturate the town each year.

Forks has deep roots in the logging industry and is the home of the largest and most complete logging museum on the peninsula. The log cabin museum, built by a local high school carpentry class in the late 1990s, includes a replica of a typical lumberjack bunkhouse and tools of the trade such as crosscut saws and chainsaws.

The first European settlers arrived in Forks, then called Forks Prairie, in 1870. Many were fur trappers who lived there part-time while they attended their traps. In 1878, the first farm family settled in the area. By the time the family arrived in Forks, they were surely exhausted from the long journey. They traveled by small ship from San Francisco to Seattle, where they boarded another small ship bound for Port Townsend. There they waited out a storm before boarding a steamer for Neah Bay,

Previous pages:
These ocean-worn logs have found their way to Kalaloch Beach. More driftwood washes up on Northwest beaches than anywhere else on Earth. These sun-bleached logs once grew in river valleys as giant conifers, such as Sitka spruce. When a heavy downpour combines with glacial melt, waterflows may rise six feet within a few hours, undermining the bank and toppling trees into the rushing torrent of the flood. The trees wash down to the river mouth and onto the beach. Other trees fall from eroding headlands while some, with numbered tags on the end, are logs that have been lost from tug-pulled log rafts.

Facing page:
A commercial fishing boat passes by James Island as it heads to sea from La Push Harbor. Home of the Quillayute Indian Reservation, La Push has been a fishing village site for at least 2000 years.

The Up Your Wind Kite Flying contest, held on Pacific Beach in early September,
attracts 3,000 people each year, including the best kite fliers in the west.
Pacific Beach, longtime home to many Quinault families, has been a popular vacation
resort since the early 1900s. The Pacific Beach Hotel, built in 1906, became known as one
of the Northwest's most popular honeymoon hotels. The hotel prospered until the outbreak
of World War II, when the Navy and Air Force converted it to their regional headquarters.
The Pacific Beach Hotel still remains but is not open to the public.

only to wait for another storm to pass. When the winds died down, they traveled by dugout canoe to La Push, a fourteen-hour trip, probably in the rain. Finally, they hiked with their belongings the last fifteen miles to their new home.

Ocean Shores

Ocean Shores is an eight-mile-long peninsula that stretches southward from the north end of Grays Harbor. The town of Ocean Shores, a recreational hot spot with few year-round residents, is located on the peninsula. There is a higher concentration of hotel and motel rooms in Ocean Shores than in any other place on the Olympic Peninsula. Ocean Shores is truly the product of a real-estate boom that took place on the peninsula during the mid 1960s and 1970s.

Hundreds of people arrive in Ocean Shores each year to dig for clams during the area's limited season. In a class by itself, the razor clam (*Siligua patula*) is the king. A native to coastal beaches, this delicacy is best when sautéed or used for chowder. The razor clam's thin, polished shell is in the shape of an old-time razor and is just as sharp when you break the shell. Razors are known to be tricky to catch; they use their "foot" to dig deep into the sand. A successful clam digger has to be very fast.

Grays Harbor

Three towns, Aberdeen, Hoquiam, and Cosmopolis, lie directly east of Ocean Shores at the base of Grays Harbor. In 1884, the first mill in the area was built in Aberdeen. By 1910, the three towns had grown to their present-day populations and supported thirty-four shingle and lumber mills. Today there are only eleven mills in the area producing pulp, paper, dimension lumber, and cedar shakes.

Many Victorian homes were built during the boom days of logging, and the residential sections of these towns, particularly the homes in Aberdeen, exhibit architecture reflective of their old-world origins. Hoquiam's Castle, formerly the home of Robert Lytle who operated one of Hoquiam's most successful lumbering operations, is a fine example. Henry H. Richardson designed the house in the uncluttered Chicago style of architecture for which he was well known. Today, Hoquiam's Castle is one of the best bed and breakfasts in the Northwest.

Grays Harbor Historical Seaport, a former shipyard and lumber mill, is now a maritime museum. The seaport features exhibits about the shipbuilding process and a replica of Captain Robert Gray's ship, the *Columbia Rediviva,* on which he explored the Northwest coast and staked the United States' claim to the Oregon country in 1792.

Fishing floats are a much-prized souvenir of a trip to the beach. They are used to keep fishing nets from sinking and to mark crab pot locations. The floats frequently cut loose in storms and rough weather. Most of the floats that are found are from fishing boats right off the coast of Washington and Oregon. But sometimes the floats that wash up on the peninsula beaches have come from as far away as Japan.

The quiet little harbor of La Push is part of the Quillayute Indian Reservation.

Ruby Beach is probably the most popular of the wilderness beaches, primarily because it is located right on U.S. Highway 101 and it features large sea stacks close to shore.

Tidal currents leave unique patterns in the sand as they recede. These patterns were discovered near Pacific Beach.

A wrecked fishing boat rests in La Push Harbor on the Quillayute Reservation.

Above:

It's not uncommon to find Ruby Beach shrouded in fog anytime of the year. The weather on the Pacific coast is dominated by abundant pre-cipitation. The peninsula has cool summers and mild but cloudy winters.

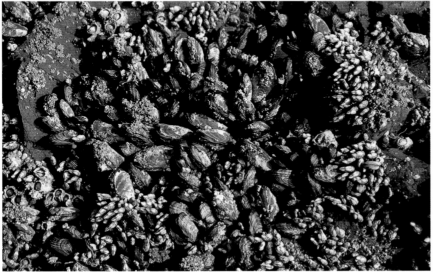

Mussels, such as these California mussels on a rock near Copalis Beach, live in a zone from the high-tide line to eighty feet below the surface, where they cling to rocks and pilings.

The opening of clam-digging season on Kalaloch Beach is quite an event. In the past, clamming seasons ran for nine months of every-day digging. Now, due to a recent decline in the razor clam populations, seasons have been reduced to as few as fifteen to thirty-five days of harvest for the entire year. The Washington State Department of Fish and Game sets open days based upon very detailed population analysis of the available legal-sized clams.

The Pacific razor clam (*Siliqua patula*) is an exceptionally meaty shellfish, which can be found along the entire western coast of the United States and Canada, from California to Alaska. It is abundant on surf-pounded ocean beaches, but also occurs in sheltered coastal areas. In Washington waters, the razor clam usually grows to a maximum, but rarely seen, length of six inches. Clams seven inches long have been recorded, but are extremely rare. The life expectancy for Washington clams is five years.

This pile of razor clams is a close representation of a daily personal limit (fifteen clams) on Kalaloch Beach. A little smaller than a dollar bill and roughly an inch-and-a-half thick, razor clams are among the most highly cherished of all Pacific seafood. Kalaloch Beach north of Olympic National Park Beach Trail 3 is home to one of only eight major concentrations of razors on the entire Pacific coast.

Kalaloch Beach is one of the best places on the peninsula to dig for clams.

Becker's Inn and Resort Cabins (previously named Becker's Ocean Resort, now Kalaloch Lodge) predates the completion of the Olympic Loop Highway by nearly ten years. Ribbon-cutting ceremonies for the new highway, now U.S. Highway 101, took place at Kalaloch in 1931. During World War II, the Coast Guard used the lodge as part of the Coastal Lookout System. The system was charged with patrolling the beaches to prevent enemy landing and to guard against communications between spies on the beach and vessels at sea.

After World War II, tourist travel on the peninsula increased, and demand for cabins and campgrounds on the coast skyrocketed. In the late 1940s and early 1950s, when Becker's Resort reverted back to recreational use, the owners improved existing buildings and constructed several new cabins. Many of the small, older cabins were moved back from the bluff at this time. Between 1950 and 1954, the Beckers erected a new main lodge and house (both are still in use today).

Above:

An equal starfish rests on a beach near Iron Springs. Iron Springs is located four miles north of Copalis Beach on the Pacific side of the Olympic Peninsula. For thousands of years, Copalis was a Native American village site; it's now a resort center.

Right:

Moclips Beach was a popular vacation resort in the early 1900s. The area was once entirely populated by the Quinault people who supported their families by spearing otters and whales from oceangoing canoes. When European hunters started settling on the peninsula in the early 1870s, the sea otter population was quickly depleted. Clams soon replaced otters as the locale's primary food supply.

At sunset, the view of the sea stacks off the Second Beach near La Push can be stunning. The 1.4-mile crescent-shaped beach is known for rough surf and great wildlife viewing. Whales, seals, and many varieties of marine birds can be seen. Marine birds are protected on the off-shore rookeries of the Quillayute Needles National Wildlife Refuge.

Above:

The wreck of the *Catala* rests at Ocean Shores.

Left:

The *Catala* was a twin-screw, 218-foot steamer built in 1925 at Montrose, Scotland. She had a long career on the Alaska run until 1950 when the Union Steamship Company was disbanded. In 1962, she was used as a hotel at the Century 21 Exposition in Seattle, then as a floating restaurant in California. After that she was towed back up the coast to be used as a salmon fishing base for sportfishermen at Ocean Shores.

On January 1, 1965, a violent storm blew in with 100-mile-per-hour winds and capsized the *Catala* at her moorings. The ship lay there for many years before the salvage rights were sold to a local firm, and the ship was demolished. Now, all traces of her have been removed right down to the sand level.

Banana slugs are so much a part of peninsula culture that the local artists use them in their work. These huge slugs are right at home at the Hard Rain Café, located near the entrance to the Hoh Rain Forest.

The annual Ocean Shores Sand Sculpture Festival is a fun event for participants and onlookers alike.

Chainsaw art is a popular event at the Ocean Shores Sand Sculpture Festival.

Above:

This beautiful nineteenth-century Victorian-style mansion, called Hoquiam's Castle, is located in the historic town of Hoquiam. Construction of this 10,000-square-foot home that overlooks the town of Hoquiam began in 1897. Lumber baron Robert Lytle completed the home in 1900. Lytle acquired his fortune from his electric sawmill, the first of its kind on the West Coast. The Lytle family lived in this unique home until they moved to Portland in 1910 and generously gave it to their niece, Theadosia Bale, as a wedding gift. It's now one of the most popular bed-and-breakfast inns in the area.

Left:

Hoquiam shipyard, on the Hoquiam River, is a busy place.

Selected Bibliography

A dandelion near the Gray Wolf River catches a ray of sunshine.

Alden, Peter, ed. *National Audubon Society Field Guide to the Pacific Northwest.* New York: Knopf, 1998.

Kirk, Ruth. *The Olympic Rain Forest: An Ecological Web.* Seattle: University of Washington Press, 1992.

Kirk, Ruth, and Carmela Alexander. *Exploring Washington's Past: A Road Guide to History.* Seattle: University of Washington Press, 1996.

Middleton, David. *Ancient Forests: A Celebration of North America's Old-Growth Wilderness.* San Francisco: Chronicle Books, 1992.

Molvar, Erik. *Hiking Olympic National Park.* Guilford, Conn.: Falcon Press, 1996.

Nelson, Sharlene P., and Ted W. Wilson. *Umbrella Guide to Washington Lighthouses.* Kenmore, Wash.: Epicenter Press, 1998.

Plumb, Gregory A. *A Waterfall Lover's Guide to the Pacific Northwest: Where to Find Hundreds of Spectacular Waterfalls in Washington, Oregon, and Idaho.* Seattle: Mountaineers Books, 1998.

Simpson, Peter, ed. *City of Dreams: A Guide to Port Townsend.* Port Townsend, Wash.: Bay Press, 1986.

Smithson, Michael T. *Olympic: Ecosystems of the Peninsula.* Helena, Mont.: Farcountry Press, 1993.

Wells, R.E. *A Guide to Shipwreck Sites along the Washington Coast.* Sooke, B.C.: R.E. Wells, 1989.

Wuerthner, George. *Olympic: A Visitor's Companion.* Mechanicsburg, Pa.: Stackpole Books, 1999.

Index

About the Author and Photographer

For thirty-three years, Seattle-based photographer Mike Sedam has traveled the world in search of the perfect picture. His work has been widely published in the travel industry and in three other books. *Olympic Peninsula: The Grace & Grandeur* is the first book Mike has both written and photographed. Mike maintains an extensive stock photography library on Seattle and the western United States, including Hawaii. To view Mike's work, visit his website at www.mikesedamonline.com.

A lonely sailboat rests in Bowman Bay near Deception Pass. The Strait of Juan de Fuca is in the background.